You can renew your book at any library or online at
www.librariesni.org.uk

If you require help please email - enquiries@librariesni.org.uk

Essential Physical Science

FORCES AND MOTION

Angela Royston

Raintree is an imprint of Capstone Global Library Limited, a company incorporated in England and Wales having its registered office at 7 Pilgrim Street, London, EC4V 6LB – Registered company number: 6695582

To contact Raintree, please phone 0845 6044371, fax + 44 (0) 1865 312263, or email myorders@ raintreepublishers.co.uk.

Text © Capstone Global Library Limited 2014
First published in hardback in 2014
The moral rights of the proprietor have been asserted.

Edited by Nancy Dickmann, Adam Miller, and Diyan Leake
Designed by Victoria Allen
Original illustrations © Capstone Global Library Ltd 2014
Illustrated by H L Studios
Picture research by Ruth Blair
Originated by Capstone Global Library Ltd
Printed and bound in China by CTPS

ISBN 978 1 406 25990 2
17 16 15 14 13
10 9 8 7 6 5 4 3 2 1

British Library Cataloguing in Publication Data
Royston, Angela, 1945-
   Forces and motion. -- (Essential physical science)
   1. Force and energy--Juvenile literature. 2. Motion --Juvenile literature.
   I. Title II. Series
   531.1'1-dc23

Acknowledgements
We would like to thank the following for permission to reproduce photographs: Alamy pp. 12 (© AC Images), 16 (© Stephen Markeson), 22 (© Fancy), 36 (© Corbis Bridge), 38 (© Marvin Dembinsky Photo Associates); Capstone Publishers (© Karon Dubke) pp. 14, 15, 24, 25, 32, 33; Corbis pp. 5 (© A2942/_ Ingo Wagner/dpa), 39 (© NASA/Roger Ressmeyer), 40 (© Jim Sugar); © Corbis p. 37; Getty Images pp. 8 (Bongarts), 18 (Neil Beckerman), 19 (Photolibrary), 27 (Chad Baker), 29 (Phil Walter), 31 (Reinhard Dirscherl), 41 (NASA); Shutterstock pp. 4 (© Ahmad Faizal Yahya), 6 (© iQoncept), 7 (© Jeff Whyte), 9 (© bikeriderlondon), 10 (© bikeriderlondon), 20 (© Maxim Blinkov), 21 (© Poznyakov), 23 (© K. Miri Photography), 26 (© Alexey U), 30 (© Jan S), 34 (© Patrick Foto), 35 (© mahout), 42 (© Denis Kuvaev), 43 (© Ahmad Faizal Yahya).

Cover photograph of tandem skydivers reproduced with permission of Shutterstock (© Atlaspix).

Every effort has been made to contact copyright holders of material reproduced in this book. Any omissions will be rectified in subsequent printings if notice is given to the publisher.

Contents

Eureka moment!

Learn about important
discoveries that
have brought about
further knowledge and
understanding.

DID YOU KNOW?

Discover fascinating
facts about forces
and motion.

WHAT'S NEXT?

Read about the latest
research and advances
in essential physical
science.

Some words are shown in bold, **like this**.
You can find out what they mean by
looking in the glossary.

How do they make that move?

A force makes something move, or changes the way it moves. When something moves, it changes position. It starts at one place and finishes up somewhere else – or it might come back to the starting point.

A skateboarder reaches the top of the ramp, spins, and lands with his feet still on the skateboard. It takes real skill to do this trick, but he couldn't do it without forces.

DID YOU KNOW?

The word *eureka* is Greek for "I have found it". An Ancient Greek called Archimedes said, "Eureka!" when he solved a problem. Archimedes solved many problems, often with the help of forces. In 212 BC the Romans attacked his home city, Syracuse, in Sicily. To defend Syracuse, Archimedes built giant **catapults**, which hurled heavy boulders with great force at the Roman ships.

Moving objects

People have invented machines to move objects more easily. Some use muscle power and some use electricity, or the force of the wind, or running water. Other forces come into play, too. Without **friction** and **gravity**, things could not slow down or fall. There would be chaos!

WHAT'S NEXT?

Suppose that a computer could pick up your thoughts and change them into actions. People who are **paralysed** may soon be helped by just such a computer chip implanted into the brain. The chip will detect thought signals and use them to guide a **robotic** arm.

What is motion?

The easiest way to describe a force is by following the way something moves. First, you need to know the object's start position, and then the position where it ended up. You can then describe the path it took to get to the end position. Some things move in an irregular path, others move in a fixed pattern.

Fixing your position

To tell someone where you are, you have to describe your position in relation to another object or your surroundings. For example, if you are meeting a friend, you might say, "I'm waiting at the bus stop across the road from school."

The green line shows the route from one place to another. This modern **software** uses GPS, just like soldiers did in the Gulf War.

Eureka moment!

How do you describe your position when everything around you looks the same? US soldiers had this problem in the desert during the Gulf War in Kuwait in 1991. Then they hit upon the solution – a **Global Positioning System (GPS)**. It used satellites in space to pinpoint their exact position. It even worked during sandstorms.

Patterns of movement

Some things move in a fixed pattern. Fairground swings move in a circle, but swings in a playground move backwards and forwards. The parts of a machine may spin, or move up and down. Mathematically, a straight line is the shortest distance between two points, but in real life, the quickest route often twists and turns around obstacles.

The swings on this fairground carousel move round in a circle as it rotates. The swings also move outwards and up as the carousel moves faster.

Getting going

You cannot move without a force to set you off. All forces either push or pull. You push a supermarket trolley, although you can also pull it. When you move a heavy table, you either lift it or pull it across the floor. Lifting is a force that pulls upwards. The heavier the thing you are lifting, the more force it takes.

A bobsleigh team pushes off at the top of the run. It takes more force to get the sleigh started than it does to keep it moving. The team runs as fast as possible before jumping onto the sleigh.

Power from afar

Most forces need to make contact. You have to hold a supermarket trolley before you can pull or push it. Other forces can pull an object without touching it. For example, a magnet pulls steel paper clips towards it without making contact. Gravity is the force that pulls everything down to the ground, whether they are touching the ground or not.

A diver leaps off the high board into the swimming pool. The force that will pull him down is Earth's gravity.

▷ DID YOU KNOW?

Gravity on other planets and moons is stronger or weaker than that on Earth. (To see why, go to page 37.) Gravity on Pluto is much weaker than on Earth. This means that if something fell onto Pluto's surface, it would fall much more slowly than on Earth.

What happens when forces clash?

A force makes a ball or other object move in different ways. It can make it change direction, or speed up, or slow down. In ball games, kicking or hitting the ball can change its direction and its speed. Putting a spin on the ball can change the direction the ball takes through the air or after it bounces.

A tennis player changes the direction of a moving ball by hitting it with a racket. If the player hits the ball so that it spins, it changes the path the ball takes.

More than one force

When a ball is hit, kicked, or thrown, several forces act on it at the same time. The force of a kick, for example, pushes the ball forward. Gravity, however, pulls it towards the ground, and the wind may slow it down or speed it up. The speed and direction of the ball is the result of these and other forces combined together.

air resistance

gravity

force of kick

The forces that act on a moving ball all affect its speed and direction.

Explaining forces

Isaac Newton is one of the most famous scientists ever. He was fascinated by what made objects change or not change they way they were moving. In 1687, he published his Laws of Motion, which explained how forces affect moving objects.

Eureka moment!

What does an object that is not moving have in common with an object that is moving in a straight line at a steady speed? Isaac Newton realized that neither object would change unless another force acted upon it. The **static** object wouldn't move and the moving object wouldn't change direction or speed.

Balanced or unbalanced?

Just because an object is static, it doesn't mean that no forces are acting on it. If both teams in a tug-of-war pull with the same force, the forces are balanced and the rope remains static. Similarly, if the forces acting on a moving object are balanced, the object will keep moving in the same direction and at the same speed. Change only occurs when the forces are unbalanced.

These teams are balanced and so the rope is not moving. If one team begins to pull more strongly than the other, the rope will move.

Pushing back

When you lean against a brick wall, why don't you fall through it? Newton's third Law of Motion gives the answer. It says that every action has an equal and opposite **reaction**. If the wall pushed back with more force, it would push you away. If it pushed back with less force, you would fall through it. Instead, the wall pushes back with the same force as you, but in the opposite direction.

Bridges

A bridge has to be strong enough to push back against the weight of all the traffic moving across it at any time. The simplest kind of bridge is a beam bridge. The more supports a beam bridge has, the longer it can be.

In a beam bridge, the weight of the bridge and the traffic is carried by the supports.

upward forces which balance the downward forces

downward forces produced by bridge and train

deck carrying railway tracks

supporting column

DID YOU KNOW?

The longest bridge in the world is the Danyang-Kunshan Grand Bridge on the railway line between Shanghai and Nanjing in China. This beam bridge is a staggering 164.8 kilometres (102.4 miles) long and has more than 2,000 supporting pillars.

Try this!

Use marbles to explore how forces make things move. Do you think that increasing the steepness of a ramp will increase or decrease the force with which a rolling marble hits a target?

Prediction

Changing the steepness of a ramp will affect the force of a rolling object.

What you need

- a pile of books about 6 centimetres (2½ inches) high
- a cardboard tube
- a measuring tape or ruler
- a drawing pin
- a large marble
- five small marbles

What you do

1. Make a pile of books 2 centimetres (1 inch) high and prop the tube against the books. Measure 20 centimetres (8 inches) in front of the end of the tube on the carpet and press in the drawing pin to mark the spot. Place a small marble as a target next to the pin.

2. Put a large marble at the top of the tube and let go. Keep trying until you hit the target full on. Measure the distance between the small (target) marble and the pin to see how far it rolled. Record your results.

3 Increase the pile of books to 4 centimetres (1½ inches) high. Do you think the target marble will roll further, the same, or less far this time? To make the test fair, you should try to hit the marble full on, in the same way as in step 2. Measure how far the target marble rolls and record your result. Was your prediction correct?

4 Increase the pile of books to 6 centimetres (2½ inches) high. How far do you think the target marble will roll this time? Make a graph of the results for the different heights of the pile of books.

Conclusion

As the ramp became steeper, the marble rolled faster and hit the target with greater force. This made the target marble roll further.

From a small force into a large force

A machine changes a small force into a large force. Some machines are very complicated, but some are so simple you probably don't think of them as machines. A lever is one of the simplest machines. It allows you to lift things that would be much too heavy to lift by yourself.

Pushing down is easier than lifting up or twisting. A lever allows the worker to turn the nut by pushing down the handle of the lever.

WHAT'S NEXT?

When you walk, you use your foot as a lever to push yourself forward. The latest running shoes are designed to help you run faster. As your foot pushes against the ground, the force squashes four **lugs** under the shoe. As you lift your foot, the force stored in the lugs is released, giving you an extra push.

How does a lever work?

A lever turns around a fixed point called the **pivot**. The simplest kind of lever is called a first class lever. The end of its handle is usually further from the pivot than the **load**. The small force needed to move the handle down a long way becomes a large force that lifts the load up a short way. The longer the handle, the heavier the load it can lift.

This is how a first class lever works.

handle

load

pivot

DID YOU KNOW?

Archimedes (see page 4) said, "Give me a lever and somewhere to stand, and I will lift the world." He would have needed somewhere to stand so that he could push down on the lever. Also, he would have needed a very long handle to lift the world!

Why do moving things slow down?

If you roll a marble across a flat floor, it soon begins to slow down and stop. Something must be slowing it down – but what? The answer is a force called friction, which occurs when one surface rubs against another. Heavy objects create more friction when they move than lighter ones.

It might sound as if friction is a nuisance, but we couldn't manage without it. Without friction, your feet couldn't grip the ground – they would slip from under you when you tried to walk. Without friction, car brakes wouldn't work.

Imagine a world with no brakes. The only way to stop would be to run into a tree or other fixed object. Luckily, we have friction!

How do brakes use friction?

To stop a bicycle, you have to slow the wheels down and stop them moving around. Brakes do this by bringing pads into contact with the wheels. This creates friction between the pads and the wheels, which slows down the wheels.

A bicycle brake contains two rubber pads, one on each side of the wheel. When the brake is pulled, the pads rub against the rim of the moving wheel.

brake pad

Eureka moment!

Leonardo da Vinci (1452–1519) was a scientist as well as a famous artist. He discovered that friction is not affected by the size of the surface areas that are in contact with each other. In other words, if you slide a large box across the floor, it won't slow down any faster or slower than a small box of the same weight and material. This is not what most people expect, but it is true for hard surfaces.

Rough and smooth

It is much easier to slide on a smooth surface, such as ice, than on a rough one. This is because smooth surfaces create less friction than rough ones. Engineers often need to reduce friction in machines, because friction wears down the parts that rub together. Friction also produces heat. Rubbing your hands together, for example, warms them up.

A snowboard slides fast down a snowy hillside. The board slides easily because the bottom of the board and the snow are both smooth.

Eureka moment!

Charles-Augustin de Coulomb lived about 250 years ago. He realized it would be useful to know how much friction different materials and surfaces created, so he designed a device called a tribometer to measure friction for different surfaces.

Making surfaces more slippery

Wet surfaces create less friction than dry ones. This can be dangerous if you are walking on a wet floor, but it is useful to engineers who want to reduce friction in machines. Engineers use oil to **lubricate** a machine. The oil coats the moving parts of the machine to make their surfaces more slippery.

Why can you slide down a water slide faster than down a dry slide? The reason is that water creates a slippery layer between you and the slide.

Get a grip!

How can you avoid slipping on wet ground? One way is to wear boots or shoes with **treads**. Treads are the squashy ridges on the soles of your shoes and on the tyres of bicycles, cars, and other vehicles.

The soles of trainers and boots are made of materials that increase friction. They also have deep treads. The treads push the water out from under the shoe so that they grip better on wet ground. Tap shoes, on the other hand, have smooth metal plates on their soles. The plates reduce friction and allow the dancers to slide their feet across the floor.

Hip-hop dancers wear shoes that grip the floor well. The soles of the shoes stop the dancers from slipping as they make their acrobatic moves.

On the road

The treads on the tyres of road vehicles grip the road, but they also slow the vehicles down. Racing cars have smooth tyres so that the riders can drive faster. If it rains, however, the wheels are changed to ones with more tread to stop them skidding on the wet road. The treads push away the water between the tyres and the road.

The treads on car tyres contain complicated patterns. Each pattern helps the car to grip the road in different weather conditions.

WHAT'S NEXT?

A new type of tyre has been developed in California in the United States. It uses electricity to adjust the depth of tread to match the weather. The tread is fairly shallow on dry roads, but becomes deep on slush and snow.

Try this!

A force meter measures the size of a force. If you want to do this experiment at home, ask your teacher if you can borrow a school force meter. You will also need to find a variety of rough and smooth surfaces.

Prediction

Less force will be needed to move objects across surfaces that create least friction.

What you need

- a force meter
- a cup
- several different surfaces, such as a wooden floor, thin carpet, sandpaper, kitchen counter
- water

What you do:

1 Place the cup on the wooden surface. Attach the force meter to the cup.

2 Pull the force meter until the cup just begins to move across the wooden floor. What force does it take? Record the result and the surface.

3 Repeat steps 1 and 2 on each different surface. Record your results for each one.

4 Wipe a small amount of water across the kitchen counter and do the experiment again. Does the wet counter produce more or less friction than when it was dry?

Conclusion
The smoother the surface, the less friction it created and so the less force was needed to move the cup.

Is resistance a drag?

Why is it harder to wade through water than to walk through air? The answer is that water pushes back with more force than air. The force is called **resistance**, or **drag**, and it is a type of friction. Air and other gases also resist movement, but not as much as liquids.

A parachutist appears to dangle in the air. The parachute creates extra air resistance, which allows the parachutist to fall gently to the ground.

Drag can be useful!

Resistance slows down a moving object and, as with friction, this is sometimes useful. Drag makes a parachute or **paraglider** fall more slowly through the air. The bigger the area pushing against the air, the greater the force of resistance.

DID YOU KNOW?

Meteoroids are rocks and dust that fall to Earth from space. Most of them never reach the ground, because they burn up as they fall through the air. These burning fragments are called meteors. The friction between the meteors and the air makes them so hot they catch fire.

Eureka moment!

In the 1970s, the US space agency NASA wanted a spacecraft that could be used many times. The scientists came up with the **space shuttle**. This spacecraft is launched by rockets, but returns to Earth like an aircraft. It has no main engine, so only air resistance slows it down as it **glides** back to Earth. At the last minute, parachutes open to reduce its speed as it lands.

A meteor streaks through the sky. It only takes a few seconds for a meteor to burn out.

Streamlined

Air resistance is useful for parachutists, but it's a headache for aircraft designers. Drag slows the aircraft as it flies through the air. This means that the aircraft's engines have to use extra fuel to produce the extra force needed to overcome drag. Vehicles that move fast are specially shaped to reduce air resistance by allowing the air to flow smoothly around them. This is called a **streamlined** shape.

A jet fighter plane is one of the fastest moving planes. The blue lines show how the air flows smoothly around its streamlined shape.

Improving the design

Designers use various techniques to make aeroplanes, fast trains, cars, and other vehicles more streamlined. They make sure that the surface pushing against the air is as small as possible – for example, by making the front pointed. They use smooth materials, and design the rest of the body so that the air flows smoothly over it. They test out small models in a **wind tunnel**. The wind tunnel mimics the effects of moving through the sky or along a track.

DID YOU KNOW?

Fast-moving animals are streamlined, too. A cheetah is the world's fastest sprinter. With its slim, streamlined body, long tail, long legs, and powerful muscles, it can run at up to 110 kilometres (70 miles) per hour. A peregrine falcon dives onto its prey at an amazing 330 kilometres (200 miles) per hour. It closes its wings to make itself ultra-streamlined.

A cyclist bends low over the handlebars and wears tight clothes. She is making herself more streamlined to reduce air resistance. Her helmet protects her head but it is also streamlined to reduce drag.

Water resistance

Water resistance is stronger than air resistance because water is **denser**, or thicker, than air. Ships and most boats are streamlined, with a long, slim shape and a pointed bow to help them cut through the water.

Some types of boat reduce water resistance further by rising partly or completely out of the water. The shape of **hull** of a speedboat makes it rise out of the water as the boat goes faster. Hydrofoils have underwater wings, or foils, that push up through the water, lifting the rest of the craft into the air.

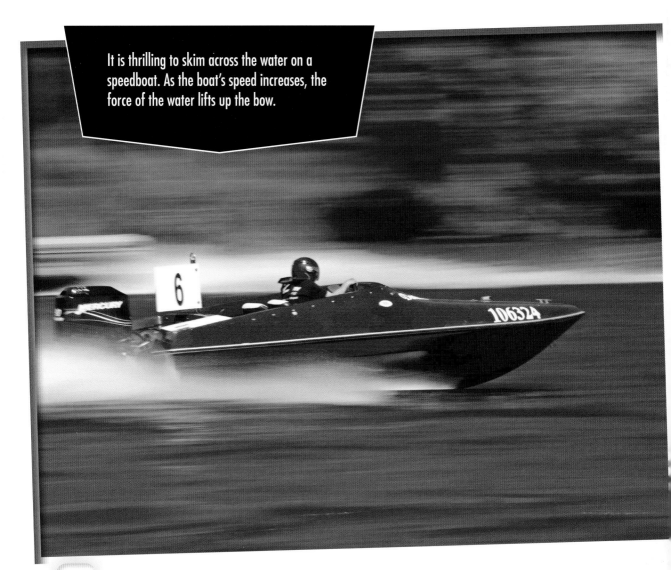

It is thrilling to skim across the water on a speedboat. As the boat's speed increases, the force of the water lifts up the bow.

The fastest swimmers

The fastest sea animals are fish, particularly sailfish, marlin, and swordfish. Their bodies are streamlined and they have a sword-shaped spike that cuts through the water. It is difficult to measure the speed of a fish, but it is thought that a sailfish can swim at 108 kilometres (67 miles) per hour.

The sailfish is the fastest-moving sea animal. It not only swims fast, but it can leap out of the water and glide through the air for several seconds.

Eureka moment!

In the 1950s, the British engineer Christopher Cockerell invented the **hovercraft**. He realized that a ship would avoid water resistance altogether if it moved over the surface of the water on a cushion of air. He tested his idea by blowing air from a vacuum cleaner through an empty cat food tin inside an empty coffee tin. The cat tin hovered!

Test out a big, medium-sized, and small parachute to find out which has the most air resistance. You will need a friend to help you time how long the parachutes take to reach the ground.

Prediction

The larger the surface area is, the greater its air resistance will be.

What you need

- a large plastic bag
- scissors and ruler
- nine pieces of string, each one 20 centimetres (8 inches) long
- three pieces of string, each one 30 centimetres (12 inches) long
- three twist ties
- three identical "parachutists" such as small plastic figures
- a stopwatch

What you do

1 Cut a piece of plastic 40 × 40 centimetres (15 × 15 inches) square. Use the scissors to make holes at the corners of the square. Thread a 20-centimetre (7½-inch) piece of string through three of the holes and one longer piece of string through the fourth hole. Tie each piece of string in place.

2 Hold the free ends of the strings together and twist the ties around them. Tie the parachutist to the longer piece of string so that it hangs below the parachute. Adjust the strings so that the parachute is balanced.

3 Cut two more pieces of plastic, one 30 × 30 centimetres (12 × 12 inches) and the other 20 × 20 centimetres (7½ × 7½ inches) square. Repeat steps 1 and 2 to make two more parachutes.

4 Ask your friend to stand on a chair ready to drop the first parachute. Say, "Go!" and use the stopwatch to time how long it takes for the parachute to drop to the ground.

5 Record the time and then test the other two parachutes in the same way. Make sure you drop each parachute from the same height above the ground.

Conclusion

Which of the three parachutes did you think would take the longest to fall? Was your prediction right?

Gravity: what's it all about?

Earth's gravity pulls everything towards the ground, but Earth is not the only source of gravity. It also exists between any two objects – and the more massive the objects, the stronger the force. The Earth is so massive its force of gravity is the only one we notice as we move around on Earth.

Gravity becomes weaker as objects move apart. Nevertheless, you would have to travel a long way from Earth before you felt any difference. Even 100 kilometres (60 miles) into space, Earth's gravity is only 3 per cent less powerful.

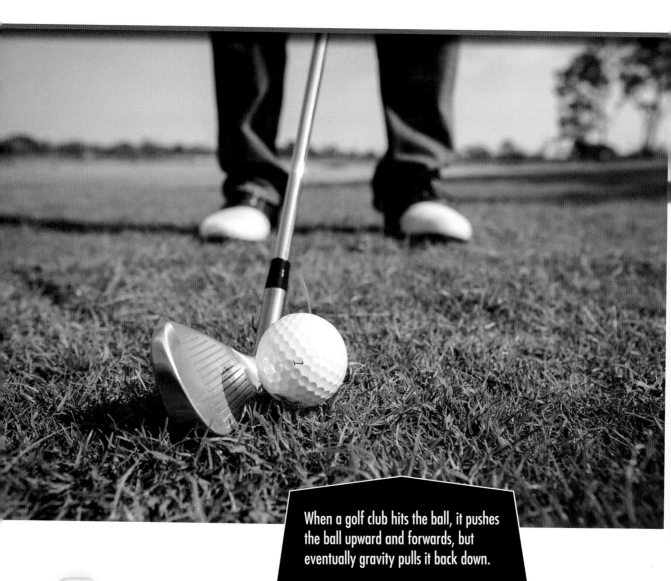

When a golf club hits the ball, it pushes the ball upward and forwards, but eventually gravity pulls it back down.

A roller coaster uses acceleration (increasing speed) and gravity to give a thrilling ride. At some points you are pinned to your seat, while at the top you feel weightless.

Eureka moment!

The pull of gravity on heavy objects is stronger than on light objects, so you might expect heavy objects to fall faster than light objects. The Italian scientist Galileo was the first person to realize that all objects fall at the same speed. He is said to have dropped a large and small cannon ball from the Leaning Tower of Pisa in 1590. They reached the ground at the same time.

DID YOU KNOW?

At some points on a roller-coaster ride, the force that drives the cars can be up to four times stronger than gravity. You feel it when the car climbs fast uphill. At the top, however, the force decreases and exactly balances gravity. Then the driving force combines with gravity to swoop you downhill.

Gravity and weight

What does gravity have to do with **weight**? It has everything to do with weight, because weight is a measure of the force of gravity. Gravity increases as **mass** increases. Mass is the amount of **matter** or "stuff" that something contains. A brick has lots of matter closely packed together. It weighs more than a pillow, which contains less matter even though it takes up more space.

This weightlifter is using the power of his muscles to lift heavy metal weights. To do this, he has to overcome the force of gravity.

Gravity on the Moon

Some planets and most moons have less mass than Earth and so their gravity is weaker than Earth's gravity. For example, our Moon has one-sixth as much matter as Earth and so its gravity is a sixth of that on Earth. If you landed on the Moon, your mass would stay the same, but your weight would drop to a sixth of that on Earth. The Moon's weak gravity would also mean you could jump six times as high!

An astronaut hops about on a Moon landing. The Moon's gravity is so weak, hopping and leaping take very little effort.

Eureka moment!

Astronaut Alan Shepard was a keen golfer. When he went to the Moon in 1971, he took a golf club and two balls with him. He realized that the Moon's weak gravity and lack of air meant he could hit the balls further than anyone had before. No one knows how far the balls actually went, but it was probably over 2 kilometres (1 mile).

Weightless in space

Astronauts in a space station move by pushing themselves off the walls and floating around. Everything else floats, too, unless it's tucked away in a cupboard or stuck in place by Velcro. The space station and everything on board are weightless, but they haven't escaped from gravity.

Astronauts on the International Space Station float and turn upside-down in mid-air. The space station is only 100 kilometres (60 miles) from Earth, so what has happened to gravity?

This astronaut is using an exercise machine in space. Astronauts have to exercise daily to keep their muscles strong.

Floating or falling?

The space station **orbits** the Earth once every 90 minutes. It travels at exactly the right speed for it to stay in orbit. If it went any faster, it would zoom off into space. If it went any slower, the force of gravity would pull it down to Earth. Instead, the space station is in a constant state of **free fall** called microgravity. Astronauts feel as if they are floating, but in fact they are falling at exactly the same speed as the space station. Everything else in the space station is in free fall, too.

▶ DID YOU KNOW?

Whenever we move on Earth, our muscles have to work against the force of gravity. In space, muscles hardly need to work at all. If astronauts who stay in space for months at a time didn't exercise, they wouldn't even be able to stand up when they got back to Earth.

What holds the Universe together?

It was Isaac Newton who realized that the force of gravity (which makes apples fall from trees) is the same force that keeps Earth in orbit around the Sun. The Sun is so massive that its gravity causes all the planets and objects in the solar system to orbit around it.

Mighty or weak?

You might think that gravity is a mighty force. In fact, scientists are surprised that gravity is so much weaker than other basic forces, such as electrical force. If it wasn't weak, however, the Universe wouldn't exist as it is. It would be difficult to move on Earth, and Earth itself would be pulled into the Sun!

This apple tree is in the garden of the Isaac Newton's house in Woolsthorpe in England. He is said to have been sitting under a similar tree, when an apple fell to the ground, and got him thinking about the force of gravity.

The Universe

The Sun is a star, and it is one star among billions that form our galaxy, the Milky Way. Gravity controls the movement of all those stars, and their planets and moons. The power of gravity doesn't end there. The Universe contains billions of galaxies, which are all held together by gravity.

The Hubble space telescope took this photograph of some of the billions of stars in the Universe.

WHAT'S NEXT?

Scientists are still trying to understand gravity. They have found a tiny **particle**, which they have called the Higgs boson, which may hold the key. Scientists say it explains why particles group together to form objects which have mass. Without mass, there would be no gravity!

Can you spot the forces?

You can see the effect of pushes and pulls, friction, resistance, and gravity wherever there is movement or action around you. For example, we can see the incredible skills and strength pole jumpers have, but forces are at work in their feats, too.

A pole jumper needs to generate a lot of force to overcome gravity and air resistance and propel herself over the high bar. Friction between her feet and the ground allows her to push off strongly without slipping. Friction also allows her to grip the pole in her hands. Air resistance slows her flight, but once she has cleared the jump, gravity pulls her safely back to the ground.

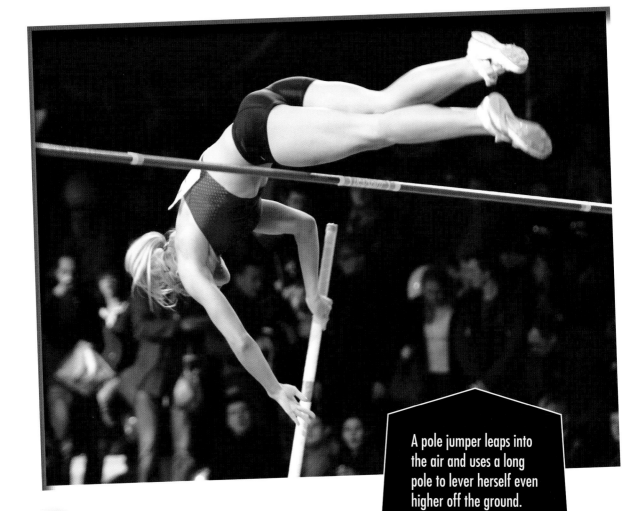

A pole jumper leaps into the air and uses a long pole to lever herself even higher off the ground.

Skateboarding

Friction and gravity have star roles in skateboarding tricks. The skateboard rolls easily, because its smooth wheels reduce friction. However, the top of the board is rough, which increases friction and allows the skater to grip the board, even in the air. Gravity helps the skateboarder roll faster down the ramp. When he reaches the other side, he jumps and spins, knowing that gravity will pull him down again.

You can't see the forces that combine to produce a spectacular skateboarding move, but you can see their result.

smooth wheels reduce friction

rough surface increases friction

treads on shoes increase friction

gravity

WHAT'S NEXT?

Inventors and engineers work constantly to invent new devices and machines that will improve the way we do things. Who knows what will happen next? One thing's for sure: if a new idea involves movement, it will involve a new way of using and combining forces.

Glossary

carousel fairground roundabout

catapult machine that throws rocks or other missiles

dense when the particles of which something is composed are packed tightly together

drag *see resistance*

free fall falling due to the force of gravity

friction force produced when one surface moves across or rubs against another

glide fly without moving the wings (bird) or without engines (aircraft)

Global Positioning System (GPS) device that uses signals from satellites in space to pinpoint a position on Earth

gravity force of attraction between two objects, but especially between an object and the Earth. On Earth, gravity pulls things down to the ground.

hovercraft vehicle that travels over the surface of the sea or flat land on a cushion of air

hull body of a boat or ship, especially the sides and bottom

load something that has to be lifted or moved

lubricate coat a surface with oil or water to reduce friction

lug part that sticks out

mass amount of matter that an object contains

matter anything that has weight

orbit travel in a fixed path around and around another object in space

paraglider large, inflatable wing, which carries a person sitting below it gently through the air

paralysed unable to move because of damage to the nerves

particle tiny piece of matter

pivot fixed point about which a lever turns

reaction force produced in response to another force

resistance force that slows down or acts against another force

robotic controlled by a computer

software computer program

space shuttle US spacecraft that looked like a huge aeroplane and returned to Earth like a glider

static not moving

streamlined has a smooth shape that reduces air resistance

treads ridges on the soles of shoes or on tyres that grip the floor or ground. Treads on tyres give more grip on wet roads by pushing the water away, and on soft or dusty roads by biting through the loose surface.

weight measure of the force of gravity on a particular object

wind tunnel large tube that mimics the conditions of moving through the air. Engineers use wind tunnels to help them design the most streamlined shape for vehicles, particularly aeroplanes, cars, motorbikes, and lorries.

Find out more

Books

A Crash Course in Forces and Motion (Graphic Science), Emily Sohn (Raintree, 2011)

Forces and Motion (Science Essentials – Physics), Gerard Cheshire (Evans Brothers, 2010)

Forces and Motion: From High-speed Jets to Wind-up Toys, Tom DeRosa and Carolyn Reeves (New Leaf Publishing Group, 2009)

The Gripping Truth about Forces and Motion (Fact Finders: Lol Physical Science), Agnieszka Biskup (Capstone Press, 2012)

Websites

www.sciencemuseum.org.uk/educators/classroom_and_homework_resources/ks2/forces_and_motion.aspx
The Science Museum website has several fun projects using forces.

spaceplace.nasa.gov/what-is-gravity
This is one of NASA's websites for children. It tells you how gravity works in space and describes its part in making the Universe as it is.

www.historyforkids.org/scienceforkids/physics/machines/lever.htm
This website gives you the history of levers, from the first animals that used them to Archimedes, and explains why they work.

pbskids.org/sid/funwithfriction.html
A game that lets you explore friction on different surfaces.

starchild.gsfc.nasa.gov/docs/StarChild/StarChild.html
NASA's website for kids includes everything you want to know about space.

www.racemath.info/Index.htm
This website tells you how friction, air resistance, opposite forces, and gravity are relevant to motor racing. Click the Key Stage 2 button for basic information and the Key Stage 3 button for further information.

Places to visit

Discovery Museum
Blandford Square
Newcastle upon Tyne NE1 4JA
This museum focuses on Tyneside in the past and the present. Its Science Maze of interactive displays includes working engines and other scientific and engineering exhibits.

Royal Air Force Museum Cosford
Shifnal
Shropshire TF11 8UP
This museum includes lots of exhibits to do with aeroplanes and flying. "The Science of Forces & Motion" is a workshop for children at Key Stage 2.

Science Museum
Exhibition Road
South Kensington
London SW7 2DD
This huge museum is devoted to science and includes Launch Pad, a hands-on gallery for children, plus galleries dedicated to flight and to space.

Playgrounds, fair grounds, and theme parks are good places to see swings, roundabouts, slides, and other examples of forces in action.

Further research

You can explore many aspects of forces and how they affect movement. Go to your local library and look for books or visit a science museum. Here are some suggestions you can research on the Internet.

Go to this website to find out how astronauts eat, drink, and wash themselves, and learn much more about what it is like to live in a space station: www.nasa.gov/audience/foreducators/teachingfromspace/dayinthelife/index.html

Find out how paragliding compares with hang gliding at:
www.extremesportscafe.com/brochure/content/what-paragliding

Find out more about how fast animals are streamlined. Search for "fastest animals" and then look for a website or a book on each animal.

Index